TO:...................................................................

FROM:.................................................................

# THE
# POWER
# OF LOVE

# THE
# POWER
# OF LOVE

SERMONS, REFLECTIONS, AND WISDOM
TO UPLIFT AND INSPIRE

# BISHOP MICHAEL CURRY

AVERY
AN IMPRINT OF PENGUIN RANDOM HOUSE
NEW YORK

AVERY

an imprint of Penguin Random House LLC
375 Hudson Street
New York, New York 10014

Most Avery books are available at special quantity discounts for bulk purchase for sales promotions, premiums, fund-raising, and educational needs. Special books or book excerpts also can be created to fit specific needs. For details, write SpecialMarkets@penguinrandomhouse.com.

ISBN 9780525542896 (hardcover)
ISBN 9780525542902 (ebook)

Printed in the United States of America
1  3  5  7  9  10  8  6  4  2

*Book design by Pauline Neuwirth*

To my wife, Sharon
my daughters, Rachel and Elizabeth
and my entire family and friends
who show me love's power every day

# CONTENTS

# INTRODUCTION

I do not actually know how Prince Harry and Meghan Markle came to the decision to ask me to offer the address at their wedding. Maybe I don't need to know.

I could well imagine the logic of it: a British prince and an American bride desire a message from some figure who represents both their worlds. They agree on the Presiding Bishop of the Episcopal Church—the United States–based church that descends from the Church of England and remains in close communion with it. There is something poetic about it: her heritage is African-American, and so is the bishop's. Here was a marriage that brought cultures together, brought countries together, brought the world together. Maybe they wanted a word from someone who understood and even represented our shared longing for reconciliation.

But I wasn't privy to their decision-making process. What I can tell you is when the Reverend Canon C. K. Robertson, my canon for ministry beyond the Episcopal Church, called to say the Royal Family would like to know if I would be available to preach a wedding on May 19, I thought he was pulling my leg. This couldn't be serious.

They were serious. This was real. Once that sunk in, I remember saying to myself, "Okay, breathe. You preach all the time. This is what you do. The gospel hasn't changed. Let it be."

So I asked the questions you ask anytime you're preparing a sermon.

First: "Who is the congregation? Who are you talking to?" Especially for weddings—and I remember this from my days as a parish priest—you always address the couple. *They* are the congregation you're speaking to. By speaking to them authentically, you end up talking to their family and friends and whoever is assembled. In this case, the assembled group was the world, but the principle still applies.

Next: "What is the gospel? What is the good news that you think Jesus is trying to say to them?" That part was surprisingly easy. They chose the biblical text from the Song of Solomon, chapter eight. Up to that point in Song of Solomon, you're reading mostly love poetry between these two people, a very real, very human love. Then, in the eighth chapter, the woman stops. She shifts and begins to realize that the love they're experiencing for each other, that love has its source in something that's bigger than the two of them. That's why the rabbis included this text in the Hebrew Scriptures. They saw the connection between the love of the two in the poem and the God who is love and is the source of all genuine love.

The miracle is that we all got to experience that love, what the text was describing. We witnessed the love of these two people. We witnessed something bigger, the source —God— while we were watching. For a while, this powerful love brought us all together: people of different political persuasions, different racial and ethnic groups, different socioeconomic groups. God used a very human love to show us a glimpse of what God's dream—God's *shalom* or peace—is for the whole world.

Whatever sermon I actually preached was only an attempt

to find words for that. I might have been preaching about the power of love, but God was giving people an experience of that power. God preached the sermon that really mattered. Our words can only point to it. You know it when you see it . . . when you're part of it.

Part of me wishes I could take the credit, but I cannot. I am glad I was sixty-five years old when this occurred. At age sixty-five, I know none of this is about me. I know the gifts I bring to the table. I also know my limits. Since the wedding, I have had surgery for prostate cancer, and felt utterly vulnerable and small in this world. That's why I can say this: everything people have said about the magic of that sermon, that wasn't me. I couldn't manufacture that. I'm not that good. I don't think anybody is. My grandmama would say, "That ain't nothing but the Lord."

All of which brings me to this moment and to this small collection of sermons and reflections. Here you will find my preferred version of the Royal Wedding address, edited lightly so that it is more suitable for reading. You will also find the first major sermon I preached after the wedding, my attempt to address the question so many people have asked:

How does anybody actually live this way of love, the way Jesus lived and taught?

I have included the sermon from our Episcopal Revival in Austin, Texas, where thousands of Episcopalians and our friends got fueled up to embrace abundant life and share more love with the world. During a public prayer and witness outside the T. Don Hutto Detention Center, I joined with hundreds of others who dared to advocate for the immigrant women held inside. Together, we applied what it means to love your neighbor as yourself, this time in a social and political context.

Finally, I have turned back the pages, to share with you the sermon that launched my ministry as Presiding Bishop, where the themes of movement, love, and transformation were already front and center.

Some experiences are such powerful messages of God's love that they become important to tell and retell, in different sermons over the years. Followers of my work may find those echoes in this collection as well. If you read this collection, maybe even pray with it, I can only hope you will come away with a renewed commitment to be people of love.

Maybe you will have a stronger, clearer grasp on what the power of love means. Maybe you will discover new ways to cultivate that way of love in your own life, so it becomes the way you live and not just a thing you do.

I hope you recognize love as the most powerful force for personal change and for changing the world around us. Yes, we live in scary times. Yes, people are hurting. Yes, people are hurting one another. But anger is not the key; revenge is not the answer. The way of love—the love and power of God—is the key to our hope and to our future.

The message of God is very simple. Love one another. Take care of one another. Take care of creation. And while you're at it, love me—love God. Do that and you will find your way. That is the core of the gospel. That is the only sermon that matters.

# THE
# POWER
# OF LOVE

# SERMONS

# THE POWER OF LOVE

### THE ROYAL WEDDING

---

### ST. GEORGE'S CHAPEL AT

---

### WINDSOR CASTLE

---

MAY 19, 2018

ON MAY 19, 2018, AN AUDIENCE OF MORE THAN one billion witnessed the wedding of Prince Harry, Duke of Sussex, and Meghan Markle, an American actress of mixed racial heritage. The first African-American head of the Episcopal Church, sister church to the Church of England, Presiding Bishop Curry was asked to preach the Royal Wedding. His theme surprised no one who had followed his preaching and teaching over the past nearly forty years: love. Between two people, between two cultures, first, last, and always: love.

From the Song of Solomon in the Bible: "Set me as a seal upon your heart, as a seal upon your arm, for love is strong as death, passion fierce as the grave. Its flashes are flashes of fire, a raging flame. Many waters cannot quench love, neither can floods drown it." (SONG OF SOLOMON 8:6 7)

The late Dr. Martin Luther King Jr. once said, "We must discover the power of love, . . . the redemptive power of love. And when we do that, . . . we will make of this old world a new world, for love is the only way."

There's power in love. Don't underestimate it. Don't even over-sentimentalize it. There's power, power in love.

If you don't believe me, think about a time when you first fell in love. The whole world seemed to center around you and your beloved. Oh there's power, power in love.

Not just in its romantic forms, but any form, any shape of love. There's a certain sense in which when you are loved, and you know it, when someone cares for you, and you know it, when you love and you show it—it actually feels right.

There *is* something right about it. And there's a reason for it. The reason has to do with the source. We were made by a power of love, and our lives were meant—and are meant—to be lived in that love. That's why we are here.

Ultimately, the source of love is God himself, the source of all of our lives. There's an old medieval poem that says, "Where true love is found, God himself is there."

The New Testament says it this way: "Beloved, let us love one another, because love is of God; and those who love are born of God and know God. Those who do not love do not know God. Why? For God is love." (1 JOHN 4:7–8)

There's power in love. There's power in love to help and heal when nothing else can. There's power in love to lift up and liberate when nothing else will. There's power in love to show us the way to live.

But love is not only about a young couple. The power of

love is demonstrated by the fact that we're all here. Two young people fell in love, and we all showed up. But it's not just for and about a young couple with whom we rejoice. It's more than that.

Jesus of Nazareth on one occasion was asked by a lawyer to sum up the essence of the teachings of Moses. He reached back into the Hebrew Scriptures, to Deuteronomy and Leviticus, and Jesus said, "You shall love the Lord your God with all your heart, all your soul, all your mind, and all your strength. This is the first and great commandment. And the second is like it: Love your neighbor as yourself." (MATTHEW 22:37–39, MARK 12:28–31, LUKE 10:25–28)

And then in Matthew's version, he added something: "On these two, love of God and love of neighbor, hang all the law, all the prophets, everything that Moses wrote, everything in the holy prophets, everything in the scriptures, everything that God has been trying to tell the world . . . love God, love your neighbors, and while you're at it, love yourself."

Someone once said that Jesus began the most revolutionary movement in all of human history; a movement grounded in the unconditional love of God for the world; a movement

mandating people to live that love, and in so doing to change not only their lives but the very life of the world itself.

I'm talking about power. Real power. Power to change the world. . . . There were some old slaves in America's antebellum South who understood the dynamic power of love and why it has the power to transform. They explained it this way. They sang a spiritual, even in the midst of their captivity. It's one that says, "There is a balm in Gilead . . ."—a healing balm, something that can make things right. "There is a balm in Gilead to make the wounded whole. There is a balm in Gilead to heal the sin-sick soul."

And one of the stanzas actually explains why. They sang, "If you cannot preach like Peter, and you cannot pray like Paul, you just tell the love of Jesus, how he died to save us all."

*That's* the balm in Gilead. This way of love, it is the way of life. They got it. He died to save us all. He didn't die for anything he could get out of it. Jesus did not get an honorary doctorate for dying. He gave up his life, he sacrificed his life, for the good of others, for the good of the other, for the well-being of the world, for us.

That's what love is. Love is not selfish and self-centered. Love can be sacrificial, and in so doing, becomes redemptive. And that way of unselfish, sacrificial, redemptive love changes lives, and it can change this world.

If you don't believe me, just stop and imagine. Think and imagine a world where love is the way.

Imagine our homes and families where love is the way. Imagine neighborhoods and communities where love is the way.

Imagine governments and nations where love is the way. Imagine business and commerce where love is the way.

Imagine this tired, old world where love is the way.

When love is the way—unselfish, sacrificial, redemptive love—then no child will go to bed hungry in this world ever again.

When love is the way, we will let justice roll down like a mighty stream and righteousness like an ever-flowing brook.

When love is the way, poverty will become history.

When love is the way, the earth will be a sanctuary.

When love is the way, we will lay down our swords and shields, down by the riverside, to study war no more.

When love is the way, there's plenty good room—plenty good room—for all of God's children.

Because when love is the way, we treat each other, well . . . like we are actually family.

When love is the way, we know that God is the source of us all, and we are brothers and sisters, children of God.

My brothers and sisters, that's a new heaven, a new earth, a new world, a new human family.

And let me tell you something, old Solomon was right in the Old Testament: that kind of love is as powerful as a raging fire.

French Jesuit Pierre Teilhard de Chardin—and with this I will sit down; we've got to get you all married—was arguably one of the great minds and great spirits of the twentieth century. A Jesuit, Roman Catholic priest, scientist, scholar, mystic.

In some of his writings, he said—as others have said—that the discovery, or invention, or harnessing of fire was one of the great scientific and technological discoveries in all of human history.

Fire to a great extent made human civilization possible. Fire made it possible to cook food and to provide sanitary ways of eating, which reduced the spread of disease in its time. Fire made it possible to heat environments and thereby made human migration around the world a possibility, even into colder climates.

Fire made it possible. There was no Bronze Age without fire, no Iron Age without fire, no Industrial Revolution without fire. . . . Anybody get here in a car today? An automobile? Nod your heads if you did—I know there were some carriages. But those of us who came in cars, fire—the controlled, harnessed fire—made that possible.

I know that the Bible says, and I believe it, that Jesus walked on the water. But I have to tell you, I did not walk across the Atlantic Ocean to get here. Controlled fire in that plane got me here. Fire makes it possible for us to text and tweet and email and Instagram and Facebook and socially be dysfunctional with each other.

Fire makes all of that possible, and de Chardin said fire was one of the greatest discoveries in all of human history.

Then he went on to say that *if humanity ever harnesses the energy of love, it will be the second time in history that we have discovered fire.*

De Chardin was right. Solomon was right. Dr. King was right: we must discover love—the redemptive power of love. And when we do that, we will make of this old world, a new world.

My brother, my sister—God love you, God bless you, and may God hold us all in those almighty hands of love.

# LIVING THE WAY OF LOVE

### OPENING EUCHARIST OF THE 79TH

### GENERAL CONVENTION OF THE

### EPISCOPAL CHURCH

AUSTIN, TEXAS

JULY 5, 2018

EVERY THREE YEARS, THE EPISCOPAL CHURCH'S leaders—bishops, clergy, and laity (those who are not ordained)—gather to pray and use the democratic process for making major decisions that shape the whole church's life. That gathering took place from July 5 to 13, 2018, in Austin, Texas. Thousands of Episcopal leaders, members, and friends came together for the Opening Eucharist, where the Presiding Bishop Curry invited the whole church to boldly live as "the Episcopal branch of the Jesus Movement"—a community of people who follow Jesus in his loving, liberating, and life-giving way, find themselves changed, and change the world. One step is to consciously take up what he calls "The Way of Love."

I

Allow me, if you will, to offer a reflection on the words of
Jesus from the fifteenth chapter of John's gospel, which happened to be at the Last Supper in John's gospel. This was not
long before Jesus' death, when he would show what love
looks like; giving of the self, even sacrificing the self for the
good and well-being of others.

At the Last Supper he says, "A new commandment I give
you." Not a new *option*, he said, but "a new *commandment* I
give you: that you love one another." At the Last Supper, he
showed them what love looked like by taking a towel and
washing the feet of his disciples. At the Last Supper, he says,
"As the Father has loved me, so have I loved you. Now abide
in my love." When he knew their world would fall apart,

when he knew uncertainty and ambiguity was in the air, when he knew that even he did not know for sure what lay ahead, and all he could do was trust the Father.

It was then that he said to them what he may be saying to us: "I am the vine, you are the branches." Have you heard it, "I am the vine, you are the branches"? Do you hear him whisper to you, the Episcopal branch of the Jesus Movement? "I am the vine, you are the branches. Abide in me and I in you, for apart from me you can do nothing. But abide in me and you will bear much fruit, and so prove to be my disciples."

Allow me, if you will, to reflect on that, the Jesus Movement text, by using another text, later in John 15. There we see another story that may illuminate what Jesus was getting at here. We may ask, "How's that, Lord? How do we abide in you and live as branches from you, the vine?" This is his answer: "By this everyone will know that you are my disciples, *that you love one another.*"

Not that you can recite the Baptismal Covenant, though that's important. Not that you know the Nicene Creed by

heart, or whichever version with the *filioque* clause or without, though that's important. Not that you know the Athanasian Creed at the end of the Prayer Book and those historical documents that only historians actually read.

No, how will the world know that you are my disciples? He says that you love one another. Love is the way. Love is the only way. Those who follow in my way follow in the way of unconditional, unselfish, sacrificial love, and that kind of love can change the world.

## II

But the question is still, How? On Wednesday I was with the Episcopal Youth Presence. We were talking about this and somebody said, "How do you follow Jesus in the Way of Love in a world that is profoundly unloving?" How do you do it? This message is for you, young people. So let me talk to them, and I want you to be like Sarah in the Bible, and eavesdrop at the tent.

First, there's an old song that may help. It says,

*I got my hand on the Gospel plow*
*Wouldn't take nothin' for my journey now*
*Keep your eyes on the prize*
*Hold on, hold on*
*Keep your eyes on the prize*
*Hold on*

Now, I have a feeling there are several passages behind that song, but one of them comes out of the fourteenth chapter of Matthew's gospel. And in the fourteenth chapter of Matthew's gospel, Jesus has sent his disciples, at least some of them, off on a trip on the sea. He tells them to get in the boat and he says, "Y'all go across to the other side. [The "y'all" wasn't in the King James Version, but that is what he said.] Y'all go across to the other side."

As they were on the perilous journey on the Sea of Galilee, in the middle of the night, if you will, a storm erupts, and they're fearful for their very lives, because this is in the middle of the night. This is night with no ambient light. This is night without artificial light. All they had, whatever lamps they had in that boat, that was it. It was *night*. James Weldon

Johnson said, "Blacker than a hundred midnights down in a cypress swamp." And they were fearful because they couldn't even see the wind and the rain, and yet they could feel them buffeting them back and forth, back and forth.

And then, when it was darkest, when it was most uncertain, Peter looked out, and he could see off in the distance, he saw a figure coming toward them. And he kept looking. He even stood up in the boat while it was rocking. Imagine the others holding on to him. And the figure kept coming closer.

At first he thought, maybe this is a hallucination. And then he could make out the face. And it was Jesus. He was walking on the water. And Peter, without even thinking, says, "Lord, if you bid me come to you, I'll come to you!" And Jesus says, "Well come on, brother." Peter jumps out of the boat and starts walking on the water, heading toward Jesus, and *he actually did it*. He just saw him, he said, "Lord!" He kept walking. "Lord! It's you!"

Then, he looked around, and it was a serious "uh-oh" moment. And the text says—Matthew very skillfully weaves the story—it says that when Peter looked at the wind and the waves and saw the storm around him and lost his focus on Jesus and focused on the storm, that is when he began to sink.

Oh, my brothers and sisters, I think there's something there. Remember the song . . .

*I got my hand on the Gospel plow*
*Wouldn't take nothin' for my journey now*
*Keep your eyes on the prize*
*Hold on, hold on*
*Keep your eyes on the prize*
*Hold on*

Oh, I bet that there's some wisdom here, because in Matthew's version, I want you to notice that the storm doesn't stop. This is not a story about Jesus calming the sea. The storm rages on. But if you want to know how to walk through a storm? Keep your eyes on the prize. Keep your eyes focused on *this* Jesus, on his teachings, on his spirit. Abide with him, dwell with him, live in him. And when you live in him, guess what? He will start living in you.

That's what's going on with Peter. That's how he does this amazing thing, walks on water. I'm not surprised that Jesus walks on the water; he is the Lord, that's what he's supposed to do—but I am surprised that Peter does it. We should look at the dynamics of how Peter does it.

Dietrich Bonhoeffer explains it for us. He was a leader of the resistance to Hitler in Nazi Germany, and died resisting that evil. He wrote a book called *The Cost of Discipleship*, and it's an exposition of the Sermon on the Mount in Matthew, chapters five through seven, where Jesus says impossible stuff like "Love your enemies" and "Bless those who curse you."

Bonhoeffer notices Jesus giving these teachings about how to live a life of love. He says, if you approach them as mechanical, legalistic things, you'll stumble. The key is not to turn the teachings of Jesus into a new law. The key, he says, is to *throw yourself into the arms of God*. Throw yourself into the hands of Jesus. And then, you might actually learn to love an enemy. Then you might pray for those who curse you. Then you know what it means to be blessed. The poor. The poor in spirit. That's what makes them compassionate.

That's what makes them hunger for God's justice. That's how Peter walks on water. To throw yourself into the arms of Jesus . . . and hold on.

*I got my hand on the Gospel plow*
*Wouldn't take nothin' for my journey now*
*Keep your eyes on the prize*
*Hold on, hold on*
*Keep your eyes on the prize*
*Hold on*

## III

Now, I'm gonna ask you to do something. Several months ago, I invited a group of Episcopalians—clergy, laity, bishops, scholars—to come and spend just a little bit of time with me. I asked them to help me think and pray through a question: How do we help our church to go deeper as the Jesus Movement, not just in word, and not just in deed, either, but for real? How do we help our folk to throw themselves into the arms of Jesus? How do you help me to do that? Because I know when we do it, and abide in him, we will bear fruit we never imagined.

But I have to admit, Michael Curry didn't have the answer. I still don't. (Yet, you're saying, what are you going to say for the rest of the sermon? Stay with me.) So we met in the Atlanta airport, because that was an easy place to be. And we just locked up, said Holy Eucharist, said our prayers, and just locked in with each other—we didn't do any wining and dining in Atlanta. We didn't go to Underground Atlanta. We didn't get any Paschal's fried chicken, though I wish we had but nonetheless, we didn't. No, we stayed there and just kept engaging, and they kept pushing me and we kept going back and forth, back and forth, and finally we realized something. We didn't need to come up with a new program for the church. We realized that—wait a minute, we don't have to do anything new.

Jesus said in Matthew's gospel, "The scribe who is fit for the Kingdom goes into their treasure box and pulls out something old that becomes something new." (MATTHEW 13:52) And we realized that we already have what we need in the tradition of the church going back centuries. For centuries monastic communities and religious communities and people who have gone deeper in this faith have lived by what they often call a *rule of life*: a set of spiritual practices that they make a commitment to live in, practices that help them open up the soul, open up the spirit, help them find their way, a way of throwing yourself into the arms of God.

They've been doing this for so long. Ask Saint Benedict, the fifth-century monk. They've been doing this a long time. We wondered, what would happen if we asked every Episcopalian to adopt what we're calling "The Way of Love: Practices for Jesus-centered Life." What would happen? And we got folk together, some of the monastic communities helped us out, some of the theological scholars and those who do formation in the church helped us out. Because we have what we need. It's sitting in this room. It's in the church. We brought them together and asked, "Help us."

And this is what they came up with. It's not a program. Did you all get these little wallet cards? Take them out. This is the old parish priest coming out in me. I always gave my congregation some homework and had a handout. Got a handout? Everybody got it? If you found it, say, "Amen!" If you can't, say, "Help me, Lord."

Look on that first page, the one that says, "What do we seek?" Now open it.

"We seek love." Because we all just want to be loved. We were made by God, whom the Bible says is love. We were made to be loved and to love.

"We seek freedom." Every child of God was meant to breathe free.

"We seek abundant life." Not bargain-basement life, but the real thing.

Maybe all that's summed up by saying, "We seek Jesus." We who are here, we have come primarily because we seek Jesus.

They came up with seven practices for living this way and seeking Jesus: Turn. Learn. Pray. Worship. Bless. Go. Rest. Those are the practices, and there're all sorts of resources online for you at episcopalchurch.org/wayoflove. This is coming from people in this church. The treasure was already here.

The practices start with *Turn*. That's *turn*, which was a nice code word for "repentance." We figured we'd scare everybody off if we started off by calling it repentance. What-

ever you call it, repentance is not about beating up on yourself; it's about turning from old ways that don't work, old habits that don't work. Turning and turning, like a flower turning in the direction of the sun. First, we turn.

Then *Learn*. As in, learn and read the teachings of Jesus in scripture daily. You know, the Bible's a good book. I don't know if it's the number one best seller on the *New York Times* list, but it ought to be the number one best seller in the Episcopal Church. I remind all my Baptist friends, we gave you all the King James Version of the Bible. We know how to *learn* from scripture.

It goes on. *Turn. Learn. Pray. Worship.* Of course! Then *Bless.* We have been blessed, in order to be a blessing. How can you bless this world, how can you bless others? Let's figure out how to bless.

Then *Go.* Go and make disciples. Go and proclaim good news. Go and be my witnesses in Jerusalem, Judaea, in Samaria, in first-century Galilee, and in twenty-first-century Austin. Go!

And then *Rest.* Sabbath rest is there in the book of Genesis for a reason. Even God had to rest.

I want to ask you to think about a commitment to a rule of life like this. I want to ask not only you but every Episcopalian to make a commitment to throw yourself into the hands of Jesus. And then live life out of that. These tools, these practices, this rule of life may help you.

## IV

Now somebody's wondering, will it work? We're not far from California, and they field-test everything in Silicon Valley. Check with the Bishop of El Camino Real or the Bishop of California; they know what I'm talking about. Everything's got to be tested. And I am glad you asked that question, because I was anticipating it. The truth is, we know it works. It's already been field-tested. Read the Psalms of David. The psalmist says, "In the morning, at noonday and at night, I offer my prayers to you" (PSALM 55:17). That is a rule of life. That is a structure of times and places and a way to pray.

Don't believe the Psalms of David? Come to the New Testament and Saint Paul. I know folk have some issues with Paul, but don't worry; my grandma used to say, "Saint Paul was like any preacher. He has some good sermons and some not so good sermons. The problem is, they put them all in the Bible." But let me tell you something, Paul was having a good day in First Corinthians, chapter nine, when he says he trains himself like an athlete. He trains his spirit like an athlete, like a great musician. He trains himself by *practicing*. Somebody asked me, how do you live a sacrificial, loving life? Well I guess it's the same way a first responder or a firefighter does. They've practiced. They've practiced how to save a life. And when the moment comes, it's instinct. These seven spiritual practices are how we practice for when the moment comes, and the Spirit moves through us.

If you still don't believe me, go back to 1963, Birmingham, Alabama. My mama's people hail from North Carolina, but my daddy's people hail from Alabama, not far from Birmingham. In 1963, the sheriff of Birmingham was a man named Bull Connor. I believe he might have been an Episcopalian, but I'm not going to investigate too much. Bull Connor's Birmingham was as segregated as segregated could be. Birmingham was seen as one of the most intractable places in the entire South. The Southern Christian Leadership Confer-

ence determined that they needed to make a stand in Birmingham in order to transform the South, and eventually the whole country.

So Dr. Martin Luther King Jr. and others went to Birmingham. The Alabama we know today is not what Alabama was then. My aunt Callie taught Sunday school in 16th Street Baptist Church in 1963. In 1963, four little girls who would have grown up to be my age were killed in that church's Sunday school when a bomb planted by a Ku Klux Klansman went off.

In Birmingham in 1963, when young people marched, the police sprayed them with water from fire hoses and German shepherd dogs attacked them.

Our own Episcopal martyr Jonathan Daniels—a white man in his twenties—gave his life in Alabama. The Alabama today is not what it was yesterday because somebody was willing to love unconditionally, unselfishly, sacrificially. And they were black and white. They were Protestant, Catholic, Jew, and Muslim. They were people of God and people of goodwill.

As part of their training for nonviolent protest, Dr. King composed a set of practices, a kind of rule of life. And here's part of what it said:

Remember, the nonviolent movement seeks justice
and reconciliation, not just victory.

Remember, always walk and talk in a manner of love,
for God is love.

Remember, pray daily to be used by God.

Remember, sacrifice personal wishes so that all might
be free.

Remember, observe with friend and foe alike, the
ordinary, normal rules of courtesy.

Remember, perform services for others and for the
world.

Remember, refrain from violence of the fist and
violence of the spirit.

Remember, strive to be in good bodily and spiritual
health.

But the first thing on the list that he repeated, over and
over again, was this:

*As you prepare to march, meditate on the life and the teachings
of Jesus.*

My brothers and sisters, I am asking us as the Episcopal Church, no . . . I am asking us as individual Christians, as the Episcopal Branch of the Jesus Movement . . . before you begin your day, meditate on the life and teachings of Jesus. I am asking you to make that commitment. Nobody's going to know but you and God, but I am asking you to make the commitment.

Before you march. While we're here at Convention, before you get up to speak at that microphone, meditate on the life and teachings of Jesus. Before you go over to the water cooler and start whispering something into somebody's ear, meditate on the life and teachings of Jesus.

When we leave this hall, meditate on the life and teachings of Jesus. When we come in here to worship, meditate on the life and teachings of Jesus.

When we go out to make our peaceful witness at Hutto Detention Center and to encourage immigrant women behind those walls, meditate on the life and teachings of Jesus. When we join with Bishops United Against Gun Violence, meditate on the life and teachings of Jesus.

Episcopal Church, join me, join me and meditate on the life and teachings of Jesus. Throw *yourselves* into his arms, and let Jesus take over.

I love this church. I was born and raised in it. Baptized on the eighth day—oh, I don't know what day it was, but anyway, baptized as an infant according to the 1928 Book of Common Prayer. Lord have mercy! My swaddlin' clothes were that Episcopal flag. I love this church, and I love it because I learned about Jesus in and through this church. And I know and I believe that we in this church can help Christianity to reclaim its soul and recenter its life in the Way of Love, the way of the cross, which is the way of Jesus.

So God love you. God bless you. Just throw yourself in the arms of Jesus and let those almighty hands and arms of love lift you.

*I got my hand on the Gospel plow*
*Wouldn't take nothin' for my journey now*
*Just keep your eyes on the prize*
*Hold on hold on*
*Keep your eyes on the prize*
*Hold on.*

# THE
# GOOD LIFE

EPISCOPAL REVIVAL AT THE

GENERAL CONVENTION OF THE

EPISCOPAL CHURCH

AUSTIN, TEXAS

JULY 7, 2018

IN 2017, BARELY A YEAR INTO HIS TERM AS THE

Episcopal Church's leader, Bishop Curry began to lead a series

of "Episcopal Revivals." While some in the culture may have

negative associations with revivals, these particular gatherings

are neither coercive nor exclusive. Local members of Episcopal

churches invite their neighbors and friends to draw together

and celebrate life with worship and prayer. They consciously

reach across racial and cultural barriers, listen to one another's

stories, commit to heal injustice and brokenness, ask for the

courage to live as witnesses to God's love in the world. The

message of abundant life and love runs through the music, the

visuals, the social media campaign, and—of course—the

preaching. More than five thousand people took part in the

Episcopal Revival on July 7, 2018, at the 79th General Conven-

tion in Austin, Texas.

O h, my Lord! Let the whole church say Amen! Say it again. Say it one more time—Amen!

This is a blessed night. Many of us gathered tonight are Episcopalians. Many of us are from other Christian traditions and families. Many of us are people of goodwill or no particular denomination or stripe. Some of us are probably Republicans. And some of us are probably Democrats. Some of us are probably Independents. But all of us are children of God. All of us! And that's what we celebrate this night. We come together as the children of God. Like that old song used to say when I was a kid,

> *Red and yellow, black and white,*
> *All are precious in his sight.*

All are precious. All!

Well, I'm in an awkward position because I have a feeling we are the only thing standing in the way of food. Allow me if you will then, to thank all of those who have made this night possible. Thanks to the bishops and people of the Diocese of Texas. Thank you, all.

I

Now, let me hasten to my text. From the New Testament, the Gospel of John, near the end of John's gospel. In fact some scholars say chapter twenty ends the gospel. But if you look in your Bible, you'll see there's another chapter. And scholars have all sorts of theories about whether chapter twenty-one is an addition, an extension, or an appendix. I'm not a scholar. I'm a country preacher, and I know preachers, and you do, too. I've got a feeling John finished his sermon in chapter twenty, the plane was landing, and he remembered something else, and he took off and came around again. That's what happened.

So on his first landing, which is chapter twenty, he almost brings it to conclusion. And he does so with these words:

Now Jesus did many other signs in the presence of his disciples which are not written in this book. But these few are written so that you might believe that Jesus is the Messiah, the Son of God, and that believing you may have life in his name. ( JOHN 20:30–31)

My brothers, my sisters, my siblings, God wants you to live. God wants us to live. God wants this world to live. You can hear it in the text. John is trying to land the plane, and he says, "There are many other things that I could've written, but I have written these few things in this Gospel that you may have life. The stories of Jesus turning water into wine, the story of Jesus meeting old Nicodemus, the story of Jesus meeting the Samaritan woman by the well, the story of Jesus feeding the five thousand folk, the story of Lazarus, the story of the crucifixion of Jesus, the story of him being raised from the dead. John could have told us more stories. This is Jesus Christ we're talking about. This brother was incredible!

John could have told stories all night. But these few stories he told so that we might come to believe. And believing means just trust. It doesn't mean you understand. It doesn't mean you got it figured out. It means I'm just going to trust you, God. These have been written so that you might believe that Jesus really is the Messiah, the Christ, the human face of God, the incarnation of God's love in the life of a human person. Or as the Nicene Creed says,

*God of God,*

*Light of Light,*

*Very God of very God*

This is not John Doe we're talking about. These have been written so that you might believe that he really is the sign, the ultimate seal of how much God loves you. And this has been written so that you can have life. Real life, not life you can barter for on eBay. Real life, life that the world did not give, and the world cannot take away. *Life.*

If you look at John's gospel, the theme of life is woven from beginning to end. It's at the beginning of the gospel with that wonderful poetry:

In the beginning was the Word, and the Word was with God. And the Word was God. In him was life. And that life was the light of the world. The light shines in the darkness, and the darkness cannot overcome it. (JOHN 1:1–5)

This is life, life with God. And it goes on. (I'm not making this up. It's in the book.) He says in the sixth chapter, "I am the bread of life." In the fourth chapter, he says, "I am the waters of life." In the third chapter, Jesus meets the first Episcopalian. I am convinced that Nicodemus in the third chapter of John was the first Episcopalian. If you read the text carefully, it says that Nicodemus was a member of the Pharisees, probably a member of the Sanhedrin, which was the high court; he was a sort of an aristocrat (smells like an Episcopalian to me). But even better than that, John's gospel says, Nicodemus came to Jesus at night. Only an Episcopalian would try to get close to Jesus when nobody was looking. That's an Episcopalian.

But Nicodemus was alright, because when push came to shove, Nicodemus defended Jesus in front of the Sanhedrin. And Nicodemus got with Joseph of Arimathea and made provision for the burial of Jesus. That's also an Episcopalian.

Why do I mention all this? It was in Jesus' conversation with Nicodemus that Nicodemus said, "You know, Lord, I want to know more about your teaching." And Jesus said to him, "Nicodemus, don't give me that jive. We're not on *Oprah Winfrey*." He said to Nicodemus, "You must be born again." In the Greek it can be translated, born again, born anew, or born from above. And the point, I think, the only reason to be born is so that you can live. God wants you to live. God wants us to have life, and God wants all of his children to have life. I could go on but I won't.

It goes on in John's gospel; he says, "I am resurrection and I am life." He says in the fourteenth chapter, "I am the way, and the truth and the life." In the tenth chapter, "I have come that you might have life." And then at the end of the gospel, "I've written all these things so that you might believe and have life." The whole point is life. Life abundant meant for each. Life for rich folk and life for poor folk. Life for Democrats and life for Republicans. Life for Independents. Life for Deputies. Life for Bishops. Life for everybody. *Life!*

## II

The truth is, it's so easy to be deceived about what makes for real life. John's gospel noticed that Jesus wasn't talking about biology. Biology is important. Because you've got to start somewhere. But that's the basics. God wants you to have life as God intended. And the truth is, I'm convinced that love is the key to that life.

I have a theory—and I know there are some theologians in this room, so I'm going to be careful—but I'm convinced that the opposite of love is not hate. The opposite of love is selfishness, and hatred is a derivative of selfishness. You see, selfishness or self-centeredness or, as the ancient mothers and fathers used to say, *hubris* (that is, false pride, self-centered pride that puts me in the center of the world, and you and God and everybody else on the periphery) . . . selfishness like that is the root of all evil. It is the source of every wrong. It is behind every bigotry. It is behind every injustice. It is the root cancer of every war. It is the source of every

destruction. That selfishness destroys homes. It will destroy churches. It will destroy nations. And left untethered, it will destroy creation. Selfishness.

And love is the cure. Love is the balm in Gilead. Love will heal the sin-sick soul. Love can lift us up when the gravity of selfishness will pull us down. Love can bind us together when selfishness will tear us apart.

There's another word for selfishness. Believe it or not, it's called *sin*. That's why we have Lent, a season to deal with sin. But love is the cure.

We've got a television show, and you know the one I'm talking about. It's the television show *Survivor*. Now it's just a television show, but think about it. The premise of *Survivor* is that you put all these people on a desert island, and the goal of their life is to find life by getting everybody else kicked off the island. That's a parable of selfishness. Because eventually selfishness gets everybody kicked off the island, and there's nobody left but you. And you are incredibly boring by yourself.

But love brings us together. Love heals the wounds. Love can lift us up. Love is the source of freedom, the root source of life. The truth is, the only reason we're here is because of love. I mean stop and think about it for a moment. We Christians believe in God. We believe in one God, and yet we believe in God the Holy Trinity. Am I right about that? We have one God and yet we know this one God as God the Father, God the Son, and God the Holy Spirit. But we don't have three gods; we have one God. We just know this one God in multiple, magnificent ways. We've got ourselves a many-splendored God.

The Holy Trinity is our tradition's way of telling us that God can embrace individuality and multiplicity all at the same time. God is not worried about uniformity. God can have unity and diversity, not uniformity, at the same time. Do you hear what I'm getting at? The truth is God has in God's own self everything that God needs to be whole and to be fulfilled, and to be complete. Saint Augustine of Hippo, no flaming liberal to be sure, once said that the Trinity means that God is a community of love in God's self.

God did not need y'all. God did not need the world and all its headaches. But love moves over and makes room and space for the other to be. Love says, let there be light. Love says, let there be a world. Love says, let there be Andy. Love says, let there be Byron. Love says, let there be Deena. Love says, let there be Hector. Love says, let there be Jeff.

First John, chapter four, verse seven, says, "Beloved, let us love because love is from God, and those who love are born of God, and know God because God is love." God is love. The reason we are here, the reason there is a world, is because God is love. We have life because of love.

Jesus said, "A new commandment I give you: that you love one another." And after he rose from the dead, he asked Simon Peter in the twenty-first chapter of John, "Do you want to follow me now?" It's not about mechanical following. He says, "Simon, son of John, do you love me?" He said, "Yeah Lord, you know I love you." "I want you to take care of my sheep. Simon, son of John, do you love me?" "Lord, I just got through sayin' I love you. Yes, I love you. You knew that." "Then take care of my sheep!" He says, "Simon, son of John, *do you love me?* If you love me, you will overcome your self-centeredness, and another will take you by the hand, and may lead you to where you do not want to go. But it won't be all about you anymore. It will be about following me."

And then Jesus said, "Now you can follow me." The key to following Jesus, the key to being his disciples, the key to life is love. It's always love.

## III

Well, I'm going to stop now. I'm getting older now. But you know the older I get, the more I am convinced that we waste a lot of time in life on stuff that does not give life. Some of that's human, and that's okay; I'm not putting all that down. But at the end of the day, we've got to *live*. We've got to live in a world where little children are not separated from their parents at our borders. We've got to live in that kind of world. And the work of love is to make a world with the real possibility of life for all. *That* is the work of love.

I really believe that's why I am a Christian, better yet why I'm a follower of Jesus. A very faulty one, by the way, but a follower nonetheless. But I am because I believe Jesus was right. The way to life is the way of love. Love the Lord your God. Love your neighbor. And while you're at it, love yourself. That's the key.

All this is predicated on a prior conviction, a conviction that God knows what God is talking about. Everything I've said is based on the conviction that Jesus knows what he's talking about. If he doesn't, then y'all might as well go eat barbecue right now.

I realized that years ago. I was a parish priest in Baltimore, and our youngest daughter, Elizabeth, was probably three years old. My wife went off to teach school, and I think our oldest daughter went off with her. It was up to me to take the young one to nursery school. So I said, "Elizabeth, I need you to go and put your raincoat on."

And she looks back at me, at three years old now. Mind you, I am the rector of St. James Church, the third oldest African-American church in the Episcopal Church. A historic church, the church that gave you Thurgood Marshall and Pauli Murray. Yes, this is a serious church, and I'm the rector talking to this little three-year-old person. I said, "Elizabeth, go put your raincoat on." And she said, "Why?"

I said, "Because it's going to rain." She ran to the window in the living room, and looked out the window and said, "But it's not raining outside." I said, "I know that, but it's gonna rain later." She said, "Mommy didn't say it was gonna rain." I said, "I know Mommy didn't say it was gonna rain, but Al Roker on the *Today* show said it was gonna rain." I tried to explain to her about weather forecasting, showed her the newspaper. And I finally said, "Why am I doing all this? Elizabeth, just go and put your raincoat on!"

She actually thought she knew better than I do. I spent more time in seminary than she's even been on the earth. And she actually thought she knew more than I did. And it occurred to me that must be what we look like to God.

I have this fantasy of God putting his hands on his cosmic hips and just saying, "They are so cute! They think they know so much, but don't they know that I was the one that called this world into being in the first place? Don't they know that I created the vast expanse of interstellar space? Don't they know that I told old Moses, Go down, Moses, way down in Egypt land, and you tell old Pharaoh, let my people go? Don't they know that I'm the author of freedom? Don't they know that I'm the creator of justice? Don't they know that I'm the God of love? Don't they know that I came down as Jesus to show them the way of love, to show them the way to life, to show them how to live together? Don't they know how much I love them?"

My brothers, my sisters, my siblings, we have work to do. To stand for Christianity, a way of being Christian that looks like Jesus of Nazareth. A way of being Christian that is grounded and based on love. A way of being Christian that is not ashamed to be called people of love. So go from this place and be people of the way. Go from this place as people of Jesus. Go from this place as people of love. Go from this place and heal our lands. Go from this place and heal our world. Go from this place until justice rolls down. Go from this place until the nightmare is over. Go from this place until God's dream is realized. Go from this place and help this world to live. "Live. *Live!*"

God love you. Now go. Go. Go!

# LOVE YOUR NEIGHBOR

## SERVICE OF PRAYER,

## WITNESS, AND JUSTICE

T. DON HUTTO DETENTION CENTER

TAYLOR, TEXAS

JULY 8, 2018

BISHOP CURRY AND MORE THAN ONE THOUSAND

Episcopalians gathered to pray and witness at the T. Don Hutto

Detention Center on Sunday, July 8. The detention center

holds immigrant women who were captured at the Mexican

border, many of them separated from their children. During the

prayer gathering, dozens of church members walked closer to

the large concrete building and chanted, "We love you! We see

you!" Several women held paper to the window; their signs read,

"Oren por nosotros (pray for us)" and "Gracias (thank you)."

efore I share just a few thoughts—and they will be just a few, we're all standing here in the sun—I want to thank all who have made this possible, especially Megan Castellan, Bishop DeDe Duncan-Probe, and Winnie Varghese. I want to say a special word of thanks to this community, to those who have helped to get permits so that we might make our witness of prayer and faith in decency and in order. And thank you to the Mayor and the Mayor Pro Tempore who came to welcome us.

Allow me to begin by saying we do not come in hatred. We do not come in bigotry. We do not come to put anybody down. We come to lift everybody up. We come in love. We come in love because we follow Jesus. And Jesus taught us love. Love the Lord your God. And love your neighbor.

Love your liberal neighbor. Love your conservative neighbor.

Love your Democratic neighbor. Love your Republican neighbor. Love your Independent neighbor.

Love your neighbor who you don't like. Love the neighbor you disagree with.

Love your Christian neighbor. Love your Muslim neighbor. Love your Jewish neighbor.

Love your Palestinian neighbor. Love your Israeli neighbor.

Love your refugee neighbor. Love your immigrant neighbor.

Love the prison guard neighbor. *Love your neighbor.*

We come in love. I would submit that the teaching of Jesus to love God and love our neighbor is at the core and the heart of what it means to be a follower of Jesus Christ. And we must be people who reclaim Christianity from its popular modality, from the way it is often perceived and presented, to a way of Christianity that looks something like Jesus. And Jesus said, Love God and love your neighbor, so we come in love.

That is the core of our faith. That is the heart of it. And we come, because we are Christian and the way of love calls for us to be humanitarian. It calls for us to care for those who have no one to care for them.

We also come because we don't believe that a great nation like this one separates children from their families. We come because we believe President Abraham Lincoln, who said this nation was conceived in liberty and dedicated to the proposition that all people are created equal. We believe that we must call this nation, America, back to its very soul.

We are here because we love this nation. Because if you really love somebody, you don't leave them the way they are. You help them to become their best selves. We are here to save the soul of America.

Now let me unpack it briefly this way. If you want a symbol for America, fly into New York City sometime. If you fly over the harbor, and I do it all the time, usually because I'm coming from Raleigh, North Carolina . . . I have to look out the left side of the airplane, and when I do as the plane is making its approach into LaGuardia airport, I see a large green statue. It is a statue of a woman and she has a torch in her hand, lifted up, and a book in her hand, and on that book are inscribed the words "July 4th 1776."

We must save the soul of America by calling America back to its core, to its core values, which it hasn't always lived up to, but the values are there nonetheless. And on July 4, 1776, if I remember my history correctly, on that day was issued a Declaration of Independence. We're friends with Great Britain now, but back then we had some issues. On that day, in the Declaration of Independence, our founders wrote, "We hold these truths to be self-evident, that all men"—all people, all people—"are created equal."

Not just American people, no, but all people, wherever they come from. People from Honduras, people from Mexico, people from Costa Rica, people from Venezuela, people from Asia, people from Africa, people from Europe, all people are created equal. *All.*

Now I think that's America. And then the text goes on in the Declaration of Independence, that all people are created equal: "they are endowed by their Creator"—not by Congress, not by a parliament, not by a potentate, not by a president, endowed by the Creator. They are endowed "with

certain unalienable Rights," rights that cannot be abridged or cannot be amended because they derive from God. What are those rights? To life, liberty, and the pursuit of happiness. *That* is the American way.

We come in love. We come because we believe in loving your neighbor. And we come because we love America, and we want America to be true to her highest self.

Let me go on. On that same Statue of Liberty there is a poem that was composed by Emma Lazarus. Hear me now: these are the words on the Statue of Liberty. You can't get more American than that. So, America, hear me well. On the Statue of Liberty these are the words:

*Not like the brazen giant of Greek fame,*
*With conquering limbs astride from land to land;*
*Here at our sea-washed, sunset gates shall stand*
*A mighty woman with a torch, whose flame*
*Is the imprisoned lightning, and her name—*

Hear me, America:

*Her name*

*Mother of Exiles. From her beacon-hand*

*Glows world-wide welcome; her mild eyes command*

*The air-bridged harbor that twin cities frame.*

And this is what she says:

*"Keep, ancient lands, your storied pomp!" cries she*

*With silent lips. "Give me your tired, your poor,*

*Your huddled masses yearning to breathe free,*

*The wretched refuse of your teeming shore.*

*Send these, the homeless, the tempest-tost to me,*

*I lift my lamp before the golden door!"*

America. *America* means "welcome." Come, God's children. *America* means "welcome." We come because we are people of love. We love those who seek refuge from war and violence and hardship. We come because we want America to truly be great.

Alexis de Tocqueville came and spent time in the United States in the nineteenth century. He traveled the land and

met and listened to the peoples. He listened to the indigenous people of the land. The other people who weren't indigenous, or natives, the rest who had immigrated to the land—help me, somebody—all the folk he got to meet. He met slaves and free slaves, met European Americans who had come here, fleeing famine, fleeing persecution. He met the peoples of America, and de Tocqueville wrote, and I quote, "America is great because America is good."

Let us make America great again, by making America good, by making America kind, by making America just, by making America loving. Let us make America great again.

God love you. God bless you. And don't you quit, and don't you get weary. God bless you all!

# WELCOME
# TO THE
# MOVEMENT

WASHINGTON NATIONAL CATHEDRAL

---

WASHINGTON, D.C.

ALL SAINTS' DAY

NOVEMBER 1, 2015

BISHOP CURRY WAS OFFICIALLY INSTALLED AS THE twenty-seventh Presiding Bishop and Primate of the Episcopal Church on November 1, 2015. He is the first African-American elected to this role, serving as chief evangelist, pastor, teacher, and public leader among nearly two million Episcopalians in the United States and more than a dozen other countries. He also represents the Episcopal Church as a leader in the world-wide Anglican Communion, the community of an estimated eighty million Christians who trace their lineage through the Church of England back to the Catholic and early church. He preached this message on the occasion of his installation, laying out the themes that would shape his nine-year term.

n the Name of our loving, liberating, and life-giving God:

Father, Son, and Holy Spirit. Amen.

It is surely an understatement to say that this is a deeply complex and difficult time for our world. Life is not easy. It is surely an understatement to say that these are not, and will not be, easy times for people of faith. Churches, religious communities, and institutions are being profoundly challenged. You don't need me to tell you that.

The realistic social critique of Charles Dickens rings true for us even now. "It was the best of times, it was the worst of times." But that's alright. We follow Jesus. Remember what he said at the Last Supper, just hours before he would be arrested and executed? "In the world ye shall have tribulation; but be of good cheer; I have overcome the world." ( JOHN 16:33)

I want to talk this morning, borrowing from what might be Bobby McFerrin's paraphrase of Jesus' words: "Don't worry. Be happy!" Let me offer a text from the seventeenth chapter of the Acts of the Apostles.

When [the angry crowd could not find the Apostle Paul and Silas], they dragged Jason and some believers before the city authorities, shouting, "These people who have been turning the world upside down have come here also. . . . They are all acting contrary to the decrees of the emperor, saying that there is another king named Jesus." (Acts 17:6–7)

That was the Jesus Movement in the first century. Don't worry. Be happy!

Many centuries later, Julia Ward Howe, writing in the midst of America's Civil War, spoke of this same movement, even amidst all the ambiguities and tragedies of history. This is what she wrote, paraphrased:

*In the beauty of the lilies Christ was born across the sea,*
*with a glory in his bosom that transfigures you and me.*

*As he died to make folk holy, let us live to set all free,*
*while God is marching on.*

*Glory, glory, hallelujah,*
*God's truth is marching on.*

What was true in the first century and in the nineteenth is also true in the twenty-first. God has not given up on the world, and God is not finished with the Episcopal Church yet. We are the Jesus Movement. So don't worry, be happy!

I

The truly liberating truth is that Jesus didn't really found a religion, though religious faith is important. He didn't establish a religious institution or organization, though institutions and organizations can serve his cause. Jesus began a movement.

Actually, Jesus picked up and took the movement of John the Baptist to a new level. John was part of the movement born out of prophets like Amos and Isaiah and Jeremiah.

And their prophetic movement was rooted in Moses, who went up to the mountaintop. Jesus crystalized and catalyzed the movement that was serving God's mission in this world. The Feast of All Saints is a reminder that we stand on the shoulders of ancestors who were the Jesus Movement before us. And we are the twenty-first-century Episcopal branch of that Jesus Movement.

That's what is going on in the passage from the Acts of the Apostles—the movement. The Apostle Paul and Silas, his partner in ministry, have been preaching, teaching, and witnessing to the way of Jesus in the city of Thessalonica. While their message finds some resonance with many, it is troublesome to others. A riot breaks out because of the tensions. Our text describes those who are troubled by the teaching about The Way, as the Jesus Movement was first called.

Listen to this description of the first followers of Jesus:

These people who have been turning the world upside down have come here also. . . . They are all acting contrary to the decrees of the emperor, saying that there is another king named Jesus. (ACTS 17:6B–7)

Let me mention three things at the outset. First, notice that the activity of Paul and Silas was seen not as an isolated incident in Thessalonica, but as part of a greater movement of revolution: "These people who have been turning the world upside down have come here also." Paul and Silas by themselves might not have been of much consequence. But as part of a movement, they posed a problem.

Second, this movement was perceived as somehow reordering the way things were, "turning the world upside down."

And third, the reason the movement was turning the world upside down was because members of the movement gave their loyalty to someone named Jesus and committed themselves to living and witnessing to his way above all else. "They are all acting contrary to the decrees of the emperor, saying that there is another king named Jesus." That's what we did at the beginning of this service when, in the Baptismal Covenant, we reaffirmed our commitment to be disciples, living by and witnessing to the way of Jesus, our Savior and Lord.

The way of Jesus will always turn our worlds and the world upside down, which is really turning it right-side up. The way of Jesus is about the transfiguration of the nightmare of our world in its current state into what the late Verna J. Dozier called "The Dream of God."

That's what Isaiah was trying to tell us in Isaiah 11. He saw the dream. When God's way is our way, when God's dream happens, when the world is upside down . . .

> The wolf shall live with the lamb,
> the leopard shall lie down with the kid,
> the calf and the lion and the fatling together,
> and a little child shall lead them . . .
> The nursing child shall play over the hole of the asp,
> and the weaned child shall put its hand on the adder's den.
> They will not hurt or destroy on all my holy mountain;
> for the earth will be full of the knowledge of the Lord
> as the waters cover the sea. (ISAIAH 11:6–9)

Saint John saw in his vision of the world's end in the Book of Revelation. Exiled and imprisoned for his witness to the way of Jesus, John was caught up "in the Spirit on the Lord's day" (REVELATION 1:10). He lifted up his head, and he saw the dream.

Then I saw "a new heaven and a new earth"; for the first heaven and the first earth had passed away, and the sea was no more. And I saw the holy city, the new Jerusalem, coming down out of heaven from God, prepared as a bride adorned for her husband. And I heard a loud voice from the throne saying, "See, the home of God is among mortals. He will dwell with them as their God; they will be his peoples, and God himself will be with them; he will wipe every tear from their eyes. Death will be no more; mourning and crying and pain will be no more." (REVELATION 21:1–4)

No more war.
No more suffering.
No more injustice.
No more bigotry.
No more violence.
No more hatred.
Every man and woman under their own vine or fig tree.
The rule of love. The way of God.
The kingdom. The reign.

The great Shalom, Salaam of God.

The dream.

God is on a mission to work through "our struggle and confusion," as the Prayer Book says, to realize God's dream.

My brothers and sisters, God has not given up on the world, and God is not finished with the Episcopal Church yet. We are the Jesus Movement. So don't worry, be happy!

## II

Now I know we all thought we were coming here today, via the live-stream on the internet or here in the cathedral, for the Installation of our Presiding Bishop. I thought that, too, until I was on the plane earlier this week, flying from North Carolina to the Episcopal Church Center in New York.

And I kid you not, a thought popped into my head: "You know this is not about you." It sort of jolted me inside. A lot was going on. I was on the way to fill out employment and insurance papers. The movers were coming to Diocesan House in Raleigh. I was going to spend one last day with Presiding Bishop Katharine Jefferts Schori.

The real Michael Curry was frankly scared to death and wondering, "Did you all make a mistake?" I was stuck on a plane, strapped in by my seat belt because of turbulence on the flight, and I couldn't get off. At that moment, and I'm not trying to get mystical or anything, but at that moment something said to me, "Michael Curry, this is not about you."

I must admit that was a moment of some sweet liberation. Because it's not about me. It's about God, and it's about Jesus. It's about that sweet, sweet Spirit who will show us the way "into all the truth," as Jesus promised (JOHN 16:13), who has shown us the way to be who we really were created to be.

The way of Jesus will always turn our lives and the world upside down, but we know that that's really right-side up. Therein is the deepest and fondest hope for all creation and the human family.

Just listen to what Jesus said in the Beatitudes. What the world calls wretched, Jesus calls blessed, turning the world upside down.

Blessed are the poor and the poor in spirit.
Blessed are the merciful, the compassionate.

Blessed are the peacemakers.

Blessed are those who hunger and thirst, that God's
righteous justice might prevail in all the world.
(MATTHEW 5:3–9, paraphrased)

Do to others as you would have them do to you.
(MATTHEW 7:12)

At home and in the church, do unto others as you would
have them do to you. That will turn things upside down. In
the boardrooms of the corporate world, in the classrooms of
the academic world, in the factories, on the streets, in the
halls of legislatures and councils of government, in the
courts of the land, in the councils of the nations, wherever
human beings are, do unto others as you would have them
do unto you.

That's a game changer! As it says in our Book of Common
Prayer, "Things which were cast down are being raised up.
And things which had grown old are being made new." That
will turn things upside down, which is really right-side up.
That's what Jesus said and what the Jesus Movement is about.

# III

But the key to this turning, which is at the center of the Way of Jesus, is love. The liberating love of God is the key to the Way of Jesus. Luke's gospel tells about the lawyer who came up to Jesus one day. Great teacher, he asked, in all of the massive legal edifice of Moses, what must I do to inherit eternal life? What is the cardinal principle on which it all stands? What is the goal? What is the point of it all? In other words, what is God really getting at?

Jesus and the lawyer agree that it all comes down to this: "You shall love the Lord your God with all your heart, and with all your soul, and with all your strength, and with all your mind; and your neighbor as yourself."

This is really a stunning declaration. It's about love of God and the neighbor. If it's not about love, then it's not about God. Or, as an Episcopalian named Duke Ellington used to say, "It don't mean a thing if it ain't got that swing."

But then the lawyer says (and I paraphrase): "OK, I'll grant the point about love for God and neighbor as Moses taught.

But we need to carefully define what we mean by neighbor. Just how expansive or inclusive is this definition? This could have far-reaching impact. So, who exactly is my neighbor?"

That's when Jesus makes up a story, a parable. This guy was walking on the road from Jerusalem to Jericho. That road was known to be a pretty dangerous road to travel at night. But this guy needed to go where he was going. As it happened, he got mugged and robbed. He was beaten pretty badly and was lying on the side of the road. A priest was coming down the same road, saw him lying there, but for whatever reason, walked on by. Another religious leader from the community came by a little later, and probably for fear of his own safety, walked on by, too, leaving the guy on the side of the road.

Then this Samaritan guy came by. Samaritans were not well regarded. There was some real animosity toward them that had a long history. But ironically it was that Samaritan who actually stopped, cared for the guy, bound up his wounds, put him on his own donkey, and took him into town. Then he paid for his health care and made sure the guy was taken care of until he was well.

Jesus then asks the lawyer, "Now, who was a neighbor to the man?" By asking that question, Jesus reveals to that lawyer—and on down the centuries to us—what the love of God really looks like.

But imagine the same parable with slightly different characters. A Christian was walking the road from Jerusalem to Jericho and she fell among thieves. Another Christian came by, but passed on by. Another did the same. And still another follower of Jesus passed on by. A Muslim came by and stopped and helped her. Imagine.

It could be a young black or brown youth who is hurt, and a police officer who helps. Or the police officer hurting and the youth who helps. Imagine.

An Israeli is wounded and a Palestinian helps. A native-born citizen and a new immigrant. Whatever our borders, whatever our divisions. Imagine crossing them. Imagine love.

I say again: God has not given up on the world, and God is not finished with the Episcopal Church yet. We are the Jesus Movement. So don't worry, be happy!

## IV

Last summer, the 78th General Convention of our Church did a remarkable thing: we made a commitment to live into being the Jesus Movement by committing to evangelism and the work of reconciliation—beginning with racial reconciliation. I was telling someone about this, and they said, "Do you realize this Church has taken on two of the most difficult and important works it could ever embrace?"

Let's get real. Imagine *Jeopardy!* or another television game show. The question asked of the contestants is this: "Name two words that begin with 'E' but that are never used at the same time." And the answer? "Episcopalian" and "evangelism."

I'm talking about a way of evangelism that is genuine and authentic to us as Episcopalians, not a way that imitates or judges anyone else. A way of evangelism that is really about sharing good news. A way of evangelism that is deeply grounded in the love of God that we've learned from Jesus. A way of evangelism that is as much about listening and

learning from the story of who God is in another person's life as it is about sharing our own story. A way of evangelism that is really about helping others find their way to a relationship with God without our trying to control the outcome. A way of evangelism that's authentic to us. We can do that.

And this idea of reconciliation, beginning with racial reconciliation—really? Racial reconciliation is just the beginning for the hard and holy work of real reconciliation that seeks justice across all the borders and boundaries that divide the human family of God.

It is as the Jesus Movement, following Jesus' way, that we join hands with brothers and sisters of different Christian communities, with brothers and sisters of other faith and religious traditions and with brothers and sisters. Some may be atheist or agnostic or just on a journey, but they long for a better world where children do not starve and where there is, as the old spiritual says, "plenty good room for all of God's children."

In evangelism and reconciliation, we take on some of the most difficult work possible. But don't worry. The Holy Spirit has done this work before in the Episcopal Church. And it can be done again for a new day.

It was sometime in the 1940s, just after the Second World War. In the United States, Jim Crow was alive and well. Segregation and separation of the races was still the law in much of the land and the actual practice in other areas, even if it wasn't technically the law there.

President Franklin D. Roosevelt had only been in office just a few years before he issued an executive order desegregating the defense industries for reasons of military necessity. The armed forces had not yet been desegregated. The Tuskegee Airmen were still a unit. *Brown v. the Board of Education* of Topeka had not yet been issued. Rosa Parks had not yet stood up for Jesus by sitting down on that bus in Montgomery. Jackie Robinson was playing baseball, but Martin Luther King Jr. was still in seminary.

It was in this context that a young African-American woman and her fiancé went to an Episcopal church one Sunday morning. They were the only people of color there. The woman had become an Episcopalian after reading C. S. Lewis's *Mere Christianity*, finding the logic of his faith profoundly compelling. Her fiancé was then studying to become ordained as a Baptist preacher.

But there they were on America's segregated Sabbath, the only couple of color at an Episcopal church service of Holy Communion according to the 1928 Book of Common Prayer.

When the time came for communion, the woman, who was confirmed, went up to receive. The man, who had never been in an Episcopal church, and who had only vaguely heard of Episcopalians, stayed in his seat. As he watched how communion was done, he realized that everyone was drinking real wine—out of the same cup.

Now remember, the armed forces of the United States had not yet been desegregated. The Tuskegee Airmen were still a unit. *Brown v. the Board of Education* had not yet happened. The Montgomery bus boycott had not yet happened. Jackie Robinson was playing baseball, and Martin Luther King Jr. was still in seminary.

And these folk were drinking wine out of the same cup. The man looked around the room, then he looked at his fiancée, then he sat back in the pew as if to say, "This ought to be interesting."

The priest came by uttering these words as each person received the consecrated bread: "The Body of our Lord Jesus

Christ, which was given for thee, preserve thy body and soul unto everlasting life. Take and eat this in remembrance that Christ died for thee, and feed on him in thy heart by faith, with thanksgiving."

That part was easy. But then it was time for the cup— would the priest really give his fiancée communion from the common cup? Would the next person at the rail drink from that cup, after she did? Would others on down the line drink after her from the same cup?

The priest came by speaking these words to each person as they drank from the cup: "The Blood our Lord Jesus Christ, which was shed for thee, preserve thy body and soul unto everlasting life. Drink this in remembrance that Christ's Blood was shed for thee, and be thankful."

The people before her drank from the cup. "The Blood of our Lord Jesus Christ . . ." Another person drank. ". . . preserve thy body and soul unto everlasting life." The person right before her drank. "Drink this in remembrance that Christ's Blood was shed for thee . . ." Then she drank. ". . . and be thankful." She drank.

Now was the moment her fiancé was waiting for. Would

the next person after her drink from that cup? He watched. The next person drank. "The Blood of our Lord Jesus Christ, which was shed for thee . . ." And on down the line it went, people drinking from the common cup after his fiancée, like this was the most normal thing in the world.

The man would later say that it was that reconciling experience of Christ in the sacrament of the Eucharist that brought him into the Episcopal Church. "Any Church in which people of different races drink out of the same cup knows something about the gospel that I want to be a part of."

That couple later married and gave birth to two children, both of whom are here today, and one of whom is the twenty-seventh Presiding Bishop of the Episcopal Church.

The Spirit has done evangelism and reconciliation work through us before. And the Spirit of God can do it again, in new ways, now beyond the doors of our church buildings, out in the world, in the sanctuary of the streets, in our twenty-first century Galilee where the Risen Christ has already gone ahead of us.

Yes, the way of God's love turns our world upside down. But that's really right side up. And in that way, the nightmare of this world will be transfigured into the very dream of God for humanity and all creation.

My brothers and sisters, God has not given up on God's world. And God is not finished with the Episcopal Church yet. So don't worry. Be happy!

*(Singing)*
*He's got the whole world in his hands.*
*He's got the whole world in his hands.*
*He's got the whole world in his hands.*
*He's got the whole world in his hands.*

# ACKNOWLEDGMENTS

Thanks be to God, the source of all love and the source of our lives.

I offer most sincere thanks to the Duke and Duchess of Sussex (Harry and Meghan) as well as to Her Majesty the Queen, to the Most Reverend and Right Honorable Justin Welby, and to the Right Reverend David Conner, Dean of Windsor.

My gratitude goes to the bishop and people of the Diocese of Arizona, whom I was scheduled to visit on May 19. While I was able to tell Bishop Kirk Smith the unlikely reason for the change in my schedule, no one else could know. That didn't stop them from being gracious and generous around my absence.

My literary agent, Merrilee Heifetz, and the team at Writers House have shepherded me through a brave new world.

I cannot thank Paul Levitz enough for introducing me to Merrilee and making so much of this journey possible.

Nina Shield, Hannah Steigmeyer, and the team at Avery have been professionals from start to finish, working at lightning speed to share these words with the world.

My colleagues and entire staff have been a true inspiration and taught me so much about the way of love. I gratefully recognize the Right Reverend Michael Hunn, who prayed many years that this message might have a real hearing. And particularly for production of this book, which is making that ever more possible, I have to recognize my executive coordinator, Sharon Jones, and two of my Canons, the Reverend Canon Stephanie Spellers and the Reverend Canon C. K. Robertson, who have both labored over this manuscript.

And words fail to measure my gratitude to my family and friends and my wife, Sharon Curry, who has weathered every adventure by my side with prayer, wisdom, dry humor, and grace. She also got to personally meet Sir Elton John when she accompanied me to Windsor Castle, so perhaps now we are even.

© KARA FLANNERY

The Most Reverend Michael B. Curry is the Presiding
Bishop and Primate of the Episcopal Church. Elected in
2015, he is the first African-American to lead the denomination. He was previously bishop of the Episcopal Diocese of

North Carolina. A noted advocate for human rights and the author of several books, Bishop Curry is recognized as one of the most popular preachers in the English language. He and his wife, Sharon Curry, have two daughters, Rachel and Elizabeth. They live in North Carolina.